TALKIN' TUNA

The Wit
and Wisdom
of Coach
Bill Parcells

JEFFERSON DAVIS

ECW PRESS

CANADIAN CATALOGUING IN PUBLICATION DATA
Parcells, Bill
Talkin' tuna : the wit and wisdom of Bill Parcells

ISBN 1-55022-387-9

1. Parcells, Bill – Quotations. 2. Football – United States – Quotations, maxims, etc. 3. Football coaches –
United States – Quotations. I. Davis, Jefferson, 1962– . II. Title. III. Talkin' tuna.

GV959.P37 1999   796.332   C99-931987-6

Photos credits: Associated Press, *Parcells* pp. 4, 10, 30, Mike Powell/Allsport.
Layout by Mary Bowness
Printed by Printcrafters, Winnipeg.

Distributed in Canada by General Distribution Services,
325 Humber Blvd., Etobicoke, Ontario M9W 7C3

Distributed in the United States by LPC Group,
1436 West Randolph Street, Chicago, Illinois, USA 60607

Published by ECW PRESS
2120 Queen Street East, Suite 200,
Toronto, Ontario, M4E 1E2
www.ecw.ca/press

The publication of *Talkin' Tuna* has been generously supported by the Government of Canada
through the Book Publishing Industry Development Program. Canadä

PRINTED AND BOUND IN CANADA

Contents

First Quarter
College, NY Giants Defensive Coordinator

"I've always coached the same way. I really believe that players do what you make them do, and they don't do what you don't make them do. I teach a conservative defense — zone coverage against the pass, try to force the ball outside on the run. But to force it outside, you've got to have pursuit." —*The New York Times (NYT) 31 Dec. 81*

As Giants' defensive coordinator, Parcells commented on the offense of the Joe Montana-led San Francisco 49ers: "You can't worry about how many passes he completes. He's going to complete 65% of his passes. What you do have to worry about is how much yardage he gets with those completions. But in the NFL, you've got to stop the running game first." — *NYT 31 Dec. 81*

After molding cornerback Mark Haynes into a top-notch defender: "My feeling on players is this — if you find one thing to motivate them, that might be all you need. Mark responds to competition. The better the receiver he has to cover, the better he responds." — *NYT 31 Dec. 81*

"Coming in this year, I didn't know the players here, but they didn't know me either, and that can be a plus. I'd heard that Harry Carson would drive me nuts, but he's been a joy." — *NYT 31 Dec. 81*

Historical Note: Parcells got his nickname "Tuna" when he was a linebacker coach for New England in 1980 and felt a player was trying to pull a fast one on him: "Who do you think I am, Charlie the Tuna?" — *Sports Illustrated (SI) 14 Dec. 98*

Parcells commenting on his acceptance then turning down of an offer to be an assistant coach with the Giants because of his family's reluctance to move: "There was nothing heroic about it. I made the proper decision, the same sort of decision husbands and fathers have to make all the time. The fact that I was a football coach giving up a big football job didn't make me a candidate for the Nobel Prize." — *Parcells: Autobiography of the Biggest Giant of Them All. (Chicago: Bonus Books, 1987) (Parcells) p. 71*

On his former coaches: "Everybody who ever coached me was on me, coaching me hard. But, see, if you respect a player and he respects you, then you have a relationship, and in a relationship all commentary is allowed. I can say anything to Pepper Johnson, and he will understand where I'm coming from. Man, the things coaches used to say to me." — *SI 14 Dec. 98*

One of his former coaches yelled the following at Parcells during football practice: "Parcells, I wish you were a piece of crap out there because then at least somebody might slip on you." — *SI 14 Dec. 98*

His River Dell High School coach, and future employer at Army, Tom Cahill put his arm around Parcells after he called an audible that failed: "Parcells, you S.O.B., the next time you make a call like that, your fat ass is going to be on the bench for the rest of your career, which fortunately isn't much longer." Parcells' mother commented afterwards: "Wasn't that nice of coach Cahill to console you like that." — *SI 14 Dec. 98*

"See, whatever I give as a coach, I took as a player. It happened to me, and if it happened to me and I turned out all right, then my players can take it too." — *SI 14 Dec.98*

"I'd said no to Vanderbilt, yes to Sloan and Texas Tech. The next thing I knew, I was in the middle of nowhere — Lubbock, Texas, is the state capitol of nowhere — watching the wind blow and wondering just where the next city was exactly." — *Parcells pp. 58–59*

"I'd been a football gypsy and turned my wife and daughters into gypsies too. I'd gone from Hastings to Wichita State to West Point to Florida State to Vanderbilt to Texas Tech. Just when I thought I had a terminal case of assistantitis, I became head coach at Air Force." — *Parcells p. 2*

"It's hard to intimidate my girls. They've always been able to walk in and do it. Acclimating became second nature to them. They didn't always like it. There were tears sometimes. They did it. It has been a wealth of experience for them. Their dad was learning how to be a football coach. Hell, there's no great trick to that. His daughters were learning how to be tremendous young women." — *Parcells pp. 56–57*

"Wichita State. Hastings. West Point. Florida State. Vanderbilt. Texas Tech. Air Force. Even Greyhound doesn't give you tours like that." — *Parcells p. 31*

"I liked Peterson (Florida State head coach). I got involved with strategy at Florida State, calling defenses. Designing them. It was another small step up in responsibility. But there were times when this Jersey guy started to feel like one of those screaming good-ole-boy, southern assistant coaches. I didn't like the feeling." — *Parcells p. 55*

"I loved the whole atmosphere, the attitude of the players and coaches, the conditions, the accommodations, the *game*. Long hours? Hell, the long hours had been working at The Country Club of Colorado and coordinating swimming programs." Parcells summing up his return to the NFL after a year away from football. — *Parcells p. 83*

Parcells' first impression of Lawrence Taylor: "Hated to lose. You could see that right away. The whole notion of losing was like somebody wanting to stab him in the ear drum." "When Ray and I had our little chat at the end of the first week, I said, 'Uh, I gotta get this kid into the *game*.' Ray just gave me one of those long Perkins stares and nodded, just like I'd told him the ocean was real deep, something obvious like that." — *Parcells pp. 89, 91*

More on Lawrence Taylor: "He was as arrogant as hell on the football field; but not off it. I spent a lot of time with him — shit, I didn't have to be a genius to know that he was going to be the horse and me the world's biggest jockey — and he shut up and paid attention. Lawrence had been so damn good at Carolina that I think he was used to intimidating people. I made it clear from the start that intimidating me was just out of the question, and we've gotten along fine ever since." — *Parcells p. 90*

"I've spent some strange times in football, but the strangest were those strike weeks at Giants Stadium (1982), working on those game plans we never used. It was like being defensive coordinator in 'The Twilight Zone.'" — *Parcells p. 105*

Late in the 1982 NFL season it was revealed that, at the end of the schedule, Giants coach Ray Perkins was leaving to take over at the University of Alabama while defensive coordinator Parcells was to move into the vacant coaching position. When Parcells was quoted late in the 1982 campaign, it was noticeable that he was acting like a head coach and watching the offense as well as the defense. "After the first couple of series in a game, we make adjustments. I talk to Brian Kelley, Harry Carson, Bill Currier and Beasley Reece, the guys in the middle of the defense. Then, if stark panic has set in with the defense, I won't see what our offense is doing. If the defense is OK, I'll see the offense play. But I won't be coaching the offense in my mind. I've got enough problems of my own. I'm glad I have this time frame, these weeks before the season ends, to be analytical. That lets me approach things a little more methodically. I'm not on a deadline. When the season is over, I will sit down with the offensive players. I think I have to reassure them that there are going to be people in here who can coach them. I want to be the coach of the whole team. I think my role will be giving direction, leadership, structure, an organizational base, an emotional lift. When the season ends, I can't be defensive coordinator of the Giants anymore." — *NYT 20 Dec. 82*

"I was grateful to Perkins for taking me by the scruff of the neck and dragging me back into pro football. Now I was grateful to him for leaving the Giants." — *Parcells p. 107*

"There was a lot of screaming when he (Perkins) left the Giants for Alabama, but those people never make a peep when a coach gets fired before the end of his contract; contracts are sacred, it seems to me, as long as your boss thinks they're sacred. When the time comes that they want to get rid of you, a contract is a dishrag." — *Parcells p. 65*

"I'm not being cast into an unfamiliar area. I know what the New York media is like. I know what kinds of fans we have, what attention we get, the traditions of the franchise. It can be a culture shock for someone coming from another area of the country. For me, it's a comfortable awareness because I don't think too many things will surprise me." — *NYT 20 Dec. 82*

Commenting on the discussion he had with Giants GM George Young the day Alabama was given permission to speak to Ray Perkins about their vacant coaching position: "In retrospect, I think it was an interview of sorts. He asked me a couple of pretty direct questions. It crossed my mind that he was being reasonably inquisitive about certain things." A few days later, after Perkins' leaving for Alabama was official, Young phoned Parcells who recalled: "George said, 'I want to talk to you about the situation.' I said, 'Well I want the job.'" — *NYT 20 Dec. 82*

On why he quickly phoned Indiana basketball coach Bobby Knight: "We are the same age. The other football coaches were older. We spent a lot of time together. I used to scout for him and go on trips for him. I didn't want him to read about this in the papers. Before I told him about the Giants, he said he was about to call me to tell me the Indiana football job was open. I said: 'Under the circumstances, I'm glad you didn't. I'm going to be the coach of the Giants.'" (Parcells and Knight formed a friendship in the late 1960's at West Point when Parcells was the linebackers football coach and Knight was the head coach of the basketball team.) — *NYT 20 Dec. 82*

"I think Bob Knight and I hit it off because he liked football so much and I liked basketball so much." — *Parcells p. 43*

"He's winning twenty with the guys he's getting at Army. Wait until the sides are *even*." Parcells' tribute to Bobby Knight's successful coaching. — *Parcells p. 46*

"If it wasn't for Ray Perkins, I wouldn't have a chance to be where I am. He told me when he brought me here: 'The defense is your deal. I'll do anything I can to support you.'" "When we finally got it going, I think we even changed the style of our offense to take advantage of how the defense was playing. Ray would ask me before a game, 'Can we stop these guys?' I would say, 'I think we can' or 'It's going to be a struggle.' If I thought we would have a struggle, our offense might play ball control. If I thought we could stop the other team, our offense might open up and gamble." — *NYT 20 Dec. 82*

"If a guy is willing to play hard and work hard, he is being honest. That's all I want. They know when I'm serious. I come into a room and they can tell from the way I walk in and from my first sentence what the tempo of this day is going to be. We have a lot of fun. But Harry Carson was quoted the other day as saying that I know how to smile and I know how to be serious. That's true. You've just got to be yourself. My role is changing, but that doesn't mean my personality is changing, too. I can't do that. I have a temper, but that's all just business. I let them know where they stand. I'm comfortable with the job, and I'm comfortable with me." — *NYT 20 Dec. 82*

On coping with the loss of both parents within six weeks of one another: "How do you deal with it? You just do. I spent time at the hospital, first with my father then with my mother, then with my father, and the rest of the time I tried to throw myself into my work, except that the work of finishing out 3–12–1 wasn't exactly like taking your mind off your problems." — *Parcells p. 120*

"There are a lot of things a new coach doesn't need, and a quarterback controversy is one of them. Stepping into one of those is just stepping into a pile of shit." Parcells reflecting on the difficulty of choosing between Quarterbacks Phil Simms and Scott Brunner during his first year as head coach. — *Parcells p. 114*

New Giants head coach Parcells looked back on how, as defensive coordinator, he used to motivate LB Lawrence Taylor: "After Lawrence joined the Giants, he spoke of his friend Hugh Green. So when we watched films of Green, I'd always tell Lawrence, 'Your friend Hugh Green really is terrific.' And each day I'd mention how good Green was. Lawrence wouldn't say a word. One day we were watching films in a darkened room. And I was saying how good that Hugh Green was. All of a sudden I heard a voice from the back shouting, 'If he was so good, how come you drafted me ahead of him?'" — *NYT 25 Feb. 83*

"(Brad) Van Pelt was never the most dedicated practice player of all time, but he never came up a quart low on a Sunday that I knew about." — *Parcells p. 95*

Second Quarter
NY Giants Head Coach

During his first practice as Giants head coach, Parcells said the following to the rookies and free agents who were on hand: "You're not on scholarship any more. No one's going to wake you up. But just like any other guy in a production business, I'm interested in production and reliability. I don't want guys who I have to get out of jail or don't know where they are or any of that business." — *NYT 30 Apr. 83*

Following the Giants' disappointing 3–12–1 season his rookie year, Parcells came to training camp in 1984 with a message for his team: "Everyone should watch out. My back is to the

21

wall, and everything will be different. It's no secret this is a crucial year for the Giants. You come off a 3–12–1 year, and you know changes have to happen, beginning with me, or else many of us won't be here next year, including me." — *NYT 8 Aug. 84*

During the Giants 1984 training camp Parcells noted: "Maybe the defense won't be as good. Who knows? I'll tell you this: It won't be because we don't have better athletes, because we do. I don't have a formula for success. I have one for failure — try and please everyone." — *NYT 16 Aug. 84*

Parcells' observation concerning Bears' behemoth 1st-round draft pick William "The Refrigerator" Perry, whose struggles with over-eating were well-documented: "He has rare talent. He is strong, mean and quick. If he feels like playing, nobody can block him. If he's fresh, he could be unstoppable." "I thought about him but not that high. On the second round, maybe. On the third round, sure. But first round, no. When you have problems, you don't want to have more problems." — *NYT 9 Aug. 85*

On Philadelphia Eagles' workhorse running back, Wilbert Montgomery: "Our guys called him Timex, because he could take a licking and keep on ticking." — *Parcells p. 99*

Following the Giants' 21–0 loss Chicago in the NFC divisional playoffs: "Riding home on the plane last night you think it's another off-season, another training camp, another pre-season schedule, another 16 games just to stand where you were standing yesterday. You never know when that opportunity is going to come again. We had an opportunity and didn't make the most of it." "It's been a long year. You wish it was longer." — *NYT 7 Jan. 86*

"Wild-card games and all that, I don't care about that. I just want to get in the championship game and that's all there is to it. I'm not interested in doing the job just good enough to keep it. It's too hard on me." — *NYT 7 Jan. 86*

"I learned something this year. How important it is to have some key veteran guys to help your young guys along. They not only can talk to a player harder than an assistant coach can, but they can show him. That's a great teaching aid." — *NYT 7 Jan. 86*

"I'm not going to the Super Bowl, unless I play in it." — *NYT 7 Jan. 86*

"If you don't think luck means anything in life, you haven't been paying attention." —*Parcells p. 40*

What Parcells said to the approximately 50 prospects interviewed prior to the draft: "One of the things I ask them is what the three most important things are in their life. If football isn't one of them, I worry. If a guy says the three most important things for him are his degree, job opportunities and his car, we may have a problem." — *NYT 29 Apr. 86*

Commenting on the Giants' first four draft choices being unsigned and therefore not at training camp: "They have no idea of the intensity of training camp. They have no idea of the stamina needed. Plus they've got to learn the system. So they've got three big adjustments to make, and they have to perform well enough to beat out an established player. I don't blame the players. They're just listening to someone. But they're going to be the recipients of all this. It's their job to show me what they can do. It's not my job to create jobs for them. So I'm not frustrated. I feel sorry for them." — *NYT 23 July 86*

Parcells on his version of the run-and-shoot offense: "If my quarterback runs, I'll shoot him." — *SI 22 Sept. 86*

An unknown Giants player once said: "If Parcells was named king of the world on Sunday, he'd be unhappy on Tuesday." — *SI 14 Dec. 98*

As Parcells awaited the NFC Championship vs. Washington: "Defense keeps you in the game. There are going to be some days when the offense doesn't play that well. If the defense plays well, that gives you a chance." — *NYT 11 Jan. 87*

"You're not going to be madly in love with your general manager. Coach the team. You got problems, cry yourself to sleep." — *Parcells p. 112*

"Okay: I'm guilty of being a weather fanatic on game day. *Any* game day. Two weeks before, when we'd played the Redskins in the NFC Championship game, I'd gotten to my office about the same time of day (8 a.m.) and started calling Newark Airport and the National Weather Bureau because of high winds. I wanted to know what those winds were going to be like when the ball was kicked off." — *Parcells p. 7*

Prior to the Super Bowl vs. Denver: "We're ready. They're starting to get a little irritable. You can tell they're ready. Last night, the bus drive over to the hotel was pretty quiet. Usually during the week, they're laughing, scratching, talking." "You never know what's going to happen in a game. But we haven't had any bad practices. Every day since last week, we've gotten something done. We got through practice yesterday with only one error. We missed one blocking assignment. They're loose. Guys can say what they want to say, but they'll be a little tight tomorrow. So will the Broncos." — *NYT 25 Jan. 87*

"I don't know what I expected for the locker room at a Super Bowl, but I was amazed at how tiny ours was. I sort of expected a suite at the Plaza Hotel and got the maid's closet." — *Parcells p. 8*

Parcells described a letter he sent to each of the Giants players after winning the Super Bowl: "In the letter, I told 'em that I disagreed with the idea that now that you've won, everything becomes a distraction. I encouraged 'em to take advantage of the appearances and business opportunities you're getting now. You deserve those things. That's part of your reward. I told them that all those outside things you're doing now won't keep you from winning the Super Bowl again next season. The only thing that will keep you from winning it again is not doing the things that you did last year to win it for the first time. Beginning with our conditioning program." — *NYT 23 Mar. 87*

"Right after the Super Bowl, I went to the combines (NFL scouting camps for draft-eligible players) at Indianapolis — if I hadn't, I would've felt guilty. But then I got into a little slump. I've done some things where I've wasted time. I feel guilty if I don't look at film every day. Looking at draft prospects, I really enjoy that. I think I'm out of that slump now." — *NYT 23 Mar. 87*

On the multitude of business offers that came his way after winning the Super Bowl: "I turned down almost all of them. I'll do the little radio show I did last year. I'm going to do a 10-minute TV thing each week that they can tape right here. I'm also doing a book and a couple of TV commercials, things I can get done before training camp starts. That's all. I'm not the Madison Avenue type." — *NYT 23 Mar. 87*

"The conditioning program, and the weight room, really helped with unifying the team, though I never could have seen it coming to this degree. I can walk downstairs from my office in the middle of March and find thirty-five to forty members of what you call your world champions just busting their asses, not even two months removed from Super Bowl XXI." — *Parcells p. 132*

Describing how he fulfilled a promise he made to his seven injured-reserve players to get them on to the sideline for the Super Bowl even though he soon found out it violated NFL regulations: "I arranged with my security guy, Ricky Sandoval, to let our assistant coaches on the field without credentials, then I gave the coaches' credentials to the injured-reserve guys." — *NYT 23 Mar. 87*

Referring to Phil Simms keeping himself in shape in the off-season: "I stopped worrying about him years ago. He won't stop until he retires. Besides, around here it's a short walk from Super Bowl hero to the end of a rope." — *NYT 26 July 87*

"There was a time when the Giants used to play just about all their games at one o'clock on Sunday afternoons. Now that we've won the whole thing, we've become the darlings of the networks. They want to *showcase* us in 1987. So we play three games at one o'clock. The rest of our games are in the doubleheader slot at four on Sundays, or on those new Sunday night games on Sunday night ESPN just got in the new contract, or on Monday night. Shit, we're practically a new primetime series." — *Parcells p. 166*

"It was like waiting for a decision at a fight in Las Vegas with Don King the promoter and his guy the fighter." Parcells joking about waiting for an instant replay official to make a decision. — *Parcells p. 209*

On concerns that drug testing is an invasion of privacy: "Invasion of privacy? People are *dying* out there. If you break into a burning room and a woman's dress is on fire and you got to rip the dress off to save her, you going to do it? You going to rip it off to save her life?" — *Parcells p. 154*

Despite posting a 6–3 record and holding down first place in the NFC East, many fans wondered what ailed the team. Parcells noted: "But five years ago, if we were 6–3 and leading the division, they'd be having lunches in Columbus Circle for us." — *NYT 3 Nov. 88*

Remarking on the hospitalization of Bears coach Mike Ditka: "Any of us in this business can identify with it. I drink coffee. I smoke regularly. I'm 30 pounds overweight. Real smart." — *NYT 3 Nov. 88*

Parcells relayed an old coaching rhyme: "O'er the ground the snowflakes hover, losing coaches run for cover. They never got around to winning, open season is now beginning." — *NYT 3 Nov. 88*

"We've got five or six new players who are contenders to make the team. That can turn out to be 25 percent of the defense. Right now it means one out of every four players doesn't know what's going on." — *NYT 12 Aug. 89*

Reflecting on how the dumping of the Gatorade cooler over Bill Parcells yielded millions of dollars in free TV advertising, Gatorade Vice-President John Breuer said: "It was sort of like we died and went to marketing heaven." — *Forbes 2 Oct. 89*

"The showers showed I was one of them. They weren't planned or contrived or stagy; mostly they were just fun, and I went along with it. And I went along with it because I'm one of them." — *Parcells p. 243*

Fillip Bondy of the *New York Daily News* commented on Parcells' appearance: "Bill Parcells of the Giants will forever be famous as the man who looked better dressed in Gatorade than in any jacket and tie." — *Petersen's Preview 1990*

Commenting on why he diligently scouted and drafted oversized offensive linemen: "I knew the game was changing, especially this year. There are too many multiple defenses these days, too many different fronts. You can't run eight different schemes against eight different fronts. It's too difficult to practice. You're better off just lining up with your big guys and pounding away, and then stretching the defense by throwing downfield. I knew the game would come to this someday, and I started preparing for it." — *SI 13 Nov. 89*

Referring to 1986 when they won the division and earned a first-round bye: "We won the division and had a week off before our first playoff game. I gave the players four straight days off. When we got back to practice on Thursday, Taylor's hamstring tightened up, and Simms was sore. I think if I had to do it all over again, I'd have made them work a day in there, just bring them in to run around a little bit." — *Newsday 28 Nov. 89*

When asked about an upcoming Monday night game between the Eagles and Saints that would impact on the Giants' playoff opponent: "I'll watch some of it, but if I'm tired I will go to bed. I'm not one for doing too much of that. To do that, you wind up playing the game. It's almost like you're coaching. I'm too busy coaching one team without trying to coach two teams." — *NYT 18 Dec. 89*

On former New York backup QB Jeff Rutledge, after seeing highlights of him leading the Redskins to a 41–38 win: "He always was a rally guy. Jeff always was at his best in helter-skelter games. The crazier things got, when everything was going wrong, the better he was." — *SI 12 Nov. 90*

On the well-known argument on Monday Night Football with Phil Simms after an incomplete pass on third down vs. Indianapolis: "In the defense the Colts were in, our best play was for Simms to dump the ball to Dave Meggett, but he threw to Rodney Hampton instead and the ball got tipped and fell incomplete. Now I'm mad because he didn't go where I wanted him to, but he knew if the ball wasn't tipped he would have had a first down. So now he's defending his call." — *NYT 20 Nov. 90*

On Ottis Anderson starting ahead of rookie Rodney Hampton in 1990 following the latter's solid pre-season: "You guys have Hampton in Canton already. He isn't there yet." — *Street & Smith's Pro Football (S & S) 1991*

To RB Ottis Anderson: "I tell Ottis I don't want any give-up runs. I'd rather have 15 runs full speed than 25 runs when 15 are full speed and 10 are give-up runs." — *NYT 20 Nov. 90*

Commenting on what it is like bringing the Giants into Philadelphia: "Well, when you walk out of the tunnel, you always hear some words you didn't know had been invented." — *SI 26 Nov. 90*

Late in a 7–3 loss to San Francisco, Parcells gambled and failed when he went for a touchdown to win rather than a field goal followed by a defensive stand and another field goal: "I can't do anything about that. That will be the last thing to get me down. I don't feel that anyone other than me knows what goes into a decision, why you do things. I don't feel compelled to explain it. No one can prove to me that the alternative would have worked. There are no experts who know the facts. If we don't make the play and hold them and return the punt, we're over midfield and can still score. And we could have made the touchdown in the first place." — *NYT 7 Dec. 90*

After much second-guessing of the aforementioned decision by Parcells on the local WFAN radio phone-in show: "I listen to music when I drive to work. At night, I might listen to the Knicks. But that show is show business. That show is designed to generate that. That's how they stay on the air. And a lot of people who call in have bets on the game." — *NYT 7 Dec. 90*

During a stretch when the Giants weren't playing well, Parcells told some of the players nursing injuries: "You bumps-and-bruises guys, I don't need you three weeks from now, I need you now." Soon afterwards the coach himself was hospitalized with a painful dislodged kidney stone but left early against doctor's orders: "After you say something like that, you'd better show up yourself." — *NYT 10 Dec. 90*

"Coaching is giving your players a good design and getting 'em to play hard." — *Fortune 17 Dec. 90*

Former Giants DE Jim Burt: "Bill made me feel personally responsible for every win and loss." — *SI 14 Dec. 98*

During a pre-season game with the Giants he said the following to QB Phil Simms: "Phil, you're playing great, and I couldn't ask more out of you, but on that field in about 15 minutes I'm going to give you holy hell." — *SI 14 Dec. 98*

On legendary LB Lawrence Taylor: "All you had to do was show him where the competition was. I saw the man play when he was bleeding, when he was in severe pain with a shoulder injury, when he was dehydrated. When it came to laying it on the line, there was nobody better than Lawrence Taylor." — *SI 14 Dec. 98*

After Giants' PK Raul Allegre made a 52-yard field goal in the dying seconds to beat Washington right in RFK stadium: "It was the most violent sound you ever heard. And then it stopped — dead stone silence — like you just stepped into a cemetery. And it stayed that way all across the field. All the way into the tunnel. One of the greatest feelings I ever had in my life." — *ESQ Sept. 95*

When asked about how the Giants would deal with the Buffalo Bills' record-setting hurry-up offense in Super Bowl XXV: "We're going to kick the ball. Every time it's spotted, we'll kick it." In the first half the Giants repeatedly stumbled into the ball stalling Buffalo for a few seconds and giving the New York defense a few precious moments to adjust. — *ESQ Sept. 95*

After the Giants' 20–19 win over Buffalo in the Super Bowl: "I don't know what the time of possession was, but the whole plan was to try and shorten the game for them." "God's playing in some of these games, but he was on our side this time. If these two teams played again tomorrow the Bills would probably win, 20–19." — *NYT 28 Jan. 91*

"I want size on my entire defense, not only from my front seven, but in my secondary. The defensive backs have to be physical on the receivers, jam them. Sure they'll get their share of catches, but they're going to pay for them." — *SI 4 Feb. 91*

On the morning after the Giants beat the Bills 20–19 in Super Bowl XXV: "This is what you coach for. There's no better feeling in the world." — *SI 22 Apr. 91*

Three months later he questions his desire to remain an NFL coach: "I don't really know what I want to do." — *SI 22 Apr. 91*

On stepping down as the Giants' coach after the Super Bowl win over Buffalo: "I just don't feel that I can give the same to protect the franchise the way I did. You've got to do what you think is right. To be fair to the players, it's best if someone else carries the torch for a while." — *S & S 1991*

"I don't have a crystal ball. I don't know what's going to happen. About coaching again, I don't know. Not this year. There's a big difference between trying to maintain something and trying to achieve something. I've always found that I function a lot better in achieving." — *NYT 16 May 91*

Parcells took a job as a TV analyst for NBC. He was asked about filling the competitive void in his life: "That's a good question. I really don't know. I'm hoping I can find something that challenges me. Being a coach is what I've been, so I'm not going to say I won't miss it. That's going to be hard, but I'm not going to be detached completely." — *NYT 16 May 91*

His eventual successor as Giants coach, Ray Handley, was thinking of resigning earlier in the year to attend law school. Parcells told him: "You're meant to be a coach, you should stay in coaching." — *NYT 16 May 91*

Following his official resignation as head coach of the New York Giants on May 15, 1991: "I feel like it's time." — *Newsweek (NW) 27 May 91*

While enjoying his retirement at the races in Florida: "So this is what real people do in August." — *SI 26 Aug. 91*

Third Quarter
New England Patriots Head Coach

On coming back to coach in the NFL: "It's pretty much what I thought it would be, coming back. The only difference is that when you're away, you have a tendency to think about the good things, the camaraderie, the fun. You forget about the bad — the holdouts, the controversies. You remember fast enough when you come back." — *SI 2 Aug. 93*

"In professional sports, you are what you are. Whatever you finish, that's what you are. If you're 1–15, you're a 1–15 team. If you're 2–14, you're 2–14, no better, no worse. You can look in the brochure and see that the team is 5–9, but it only lost six games by a total of nine points. You follow me? The reason the team is 5–9 is because it wasn't any good in close games. With all these sports p.r. guys, the implication is that the team just ran into some bad luck, really should have finished 9–5. That isn't the way it is in my mind. If you're 2–14, you're 2–14." — *SI 2 Aug. 93*

During training camp kicking drills in which several snaps were fired over the heads of successive punters: "Come on, snappers, centers. These punters don't play in the NBA, you know."— *SI 2 Aug. 93*

To Kevin Johnson, 4th-round draft choice from Texas Southern who was a disproportionate 6' 1", 306 lbs., Parcells said: "I'm going to be on you like a dog on a bone. You're going to be my soupbone." After this, Johnson, who never had a nickname up to this point, was known affectionately as "Soupbone" by his teammates. — *SI 2 Aug. 93*

To a TV reporter: "It's like you. What if your reporters haven't rounded up the news of the day? What if they haven't gotten the interviews? What if you haven't read the box scores of the day and you're not sure what your lead story is, and now you're going on the air in ten seconds. That's pressure, right? What are you going to do? Do you know how you're going to act?" In response the reporter quipped: "You saw last night's show, huh?" — *SI 2 Aug. 93*

When pressed about why he would risk his reputation by taking over the horrible Patriots, Parcells announced that he had "nothing to prove and no fear of the consequences." — *NW 30 Aug. 93*

Following his pre-season debut, Drew Bledsoe remarked that he was pleased with his progress. When he did poorly with his initial pass the next day at practice, Parcells snapped, "Still happy with your progress, Drew?" — *NW 30 Aug. 93*

On Drew Bledsoe adjusting to the disciplined routine of a pro quarterback: "Drew used to be an 8:30, 8:45 a.m. sleepyhead kid. Now he's in at 7:15, 7:30 every day, the way a young kid who needs to learn the game has to be. I like that." — *SI 6 Dec. 93*

Drew Bledsoe's mother approached Parcells about his confrontational approach towards coaching her son. Parcells' response? "Don't watch." — *NW 28 Aug. 95*

Espousing his belief that people are waiting to pounce if he falters: "Who cares what these idiots, some jerk newspaper guy or some guy who's on TV because he screams say? I've thought more about football in one week than they have in a lifetime." — *NW 30 Aug. 93*

Reflecting on the Patriots' 65 sacks given up the previous season: "I'll never see a team of mine give up 65 sacks. I'd slash my wrists before we have that many." — *SI 6 Sept. 93*

Prior to the AFC wild-card game versus Cleveland, Parcells reflected on the 1990 New York Giants, a team many felt overachieved in winning the Super Bowl: "That team was looked at publicly as a team that over-achieved, and I think just to the contrary. I think that was one of the very best teams. In my estimation that Giants team was and continues to be vastly underrated because of the way it played, which was grind-it-out, methodical. But it was a tremendously solid team that was capable of beating any team in a lot of years. It beat a team (15–13 in the NFC championship) that was viewed as maybe the best team in history, the San Francisco 49ers. Then we were able to beat the team with the offense of the 90's (Buffalo), that was scoring 34 or 35 points." — *TS 1 Jan. 95*

He quipped that Redskins "fans call me so many vile names it's almost respect." — *Esquire (ESQ) Sept. 95*

According to friend Ed Croke, Parcells was the anti-Pat Riley. "Pat has the hair, the suit, the look. Parcells has the styrofoam coffee cup, the doughnut, and the windbreaker." — *ESQ Sept. 95*

". . . for good luck." Parcells' reason for arranging the miniature elephants in his office so the tusks were all pointing to the door. — *ESQ Sept. 95*

On coaching young players: "Is it hard adapting to young players? Nah. I like young players. I like being with them. If you sit down, they'll tell you what's out there on the streets. I know what they feel. I'm there to help. Listen, I've seen more guys broken by the IRS than injuries. When they know you're serious, they begin to listen." — *ESQ Sept. 95*

When asked about a well-known incident when he supposedly called a reporter a moron: "I didn't say he was a moron. The question was: Did I outcoach the Jets' Pete Carroll? I said that was a stupid question and he was a jerk for asking it. He was trying to antagonize me." When asked if it was the reporter's lack of experience that caused him to ask a foolish question, Parcells answered emphatically, "No. He was a calculating guy trying to get me to yap. He was a wise guy." — *ESQ Sept. 95*

On how today's reporters read too much into things to get a story: "Look, it's much worse than it used to be. They pick you up with the camera on the sideline. They interpret your body language. They don't have a right to do that. 'Hey, he's wincing. He must be distraught.' Out-of-context sound bites. Then there's talk radio. It's like carnival barkers in the thirties." — *ESQ Sept. 95*

Why he doesn't allow his assistant coaches to deal with the media: "There's a reason. You can't have scraps of stories, ideas floating out there. It causes trouble, within and without. You can only have one voice." — *ESQ Sept. 95*

On the tensions that normally exist between a QB and a coach: "There can be a grind. But they're not privileged characters with me. They're not separate from the rest. In fact they may get it worse. Poor Phil Simms. I'd pick on him the worst 'cause he was the biggest target. We still argue on the phone." — *ESQ Sept. 95*

On Drew Bledsoe: "He's not a know-it-all kid. He has skill. But can he acquire ability? The two are confused. Ability is toughness, resourcefulness, concentration. Ability gets the jewelry. He can have the celebrity, the Nike commercials. But a champion? That's the true test. We'll see. He's just starting his journey." — *ESQ Sept. 95*

When asked to list historical figures that were of interest to him: "Churchill. Harry Truman. Tough people. But what really interests me are those sick bastards out there. Like that Oklahoma City bombing guy." "I'd hang him. In public. I believe in public hangings. But I'd torture him first. Slowly. Verrry slowly." "Sounds bad. Maybe you shouldn't use that. Lemme think about that." —*ESQ Sept. 95*

Parcells remembers his father saying: "Success is never final, but failure can be." — *ESQ Sept. 95*

"I have enough money for the first time, I'm here because I want to be." "Forget legend. I'm an ordinary guy who was lucky. That's the truth, not humility." "I gave my blood to this game. Cut me open on an operating table. I gave what I gave. But I got them, they didn't get me." — *ESQ Sept. 95*

His idea of perfect contentment: "One more point than they have." — *ESQ Sept. 95*

Commenting on a lack of role players in football: "One of the biggest problems in sports today — and not just football — is players really knowing what they are." Two years earlier he told RB Leroy Thompson who was fairly adept at running, blocking, and catching: "You can be here for five or six years if you do what I want you to do, if you take the role I want you to take. If you can do that, we'll give you a raise." Thompson responded: "I want to be the Man." Thompson never fit in with Parcells who said "If players have delusions of grandeur, they'll be the Man at home, on the sofa, watching NFL games on TV, or at the local bar." — *TS 9 Aug. 96*

After cutting veteran PK Matt Bahr: "He's the best kicker I ever had, but that's only incidental (to) how I feel about him personally." — *TS 23 Aug. 96*

Asked about rookie WR Terry Glenn's injured hamstring which Parcells claimed was a minor strain: "She's making progress." — *TS 28 Aug. 96*

Parcells apparently told Patriots WR Vincent Brisby, who was out with a pulled hamstring, that he recovered from open heart surgery faster. QB Drew Bledsoe's tongue-in-cheek reaction went as follows: "Bill's superman. He does those kinds of things. Just ask him." — *TS 26 Aug. 96*

"Once in a while we've got some brain donor out there. Every once in a while they lend their brains to someone else for about 15 minutes." — *TS 25 Nov. 96*

"This will be my last job" — Parcells after he took the New England job. — *The Sporting News (TSN) 23 Dec. 96*

On a local talk radio show in Boston: "My intention when I came here was that this would be my last job. You know, things change. I reserve the right to change my mind on anything." — *TSN 23 Dec. 96*

On the state of the New England franchise when he took over in 1993: It was "the most down-and-out, despondent, negative atmosphere you could ever imagine." — *SI 14 Dec. 98*
Parcells apparently barked the following at Patriots OL Bob Kratch who returned to the team after a 2-month battle with pneumonia: "Stop worrying about your lungs!" — *Village Voice (VV) 22 Sept. 98*

Patriots' QB Scott Zolak on Parcells' reputation for playing mind games with his players: "That stuff's overrated. The media makes more of it than what it is. There are a lot of guys here who played for him. If you interviewed them all, I'm sure you'd hear how much everybody respects him." — *The Providence Journal (PJ) 24 Dec. 98*

After the Patriots won the AFC championship: "I've tried to get them to elevate their expectations." — *Triangle Business Journal (TBJ) 17 Jan. 97*

"Be here at 9:30 tomorrow to run." Parcells addressing the Patriots after they beat Jacksonville 20–6 in the *AFC* championship. — *SI 20 Jan. 97*

On getting to the Super Bowl: "I see the faces on these players. I remember the faces of the players I had that went before. That's the priceless thing in this business. Those faces are the faces you remember. You see those kids, and there is a bond that never leaves. It's always there because we did this together. It's special. It's a little corny, but it's special." — *SI 20 Jan. 97*

Responding to the suggestion that Pats' QB Drew Bledsoe has been mediocre in the playoffs: "You've got to judge the player by where his team is. You know my old saying: 'You judge the trapper by his furs,' and he's got a couple of furs now. But, he doesn't have the biggest fur." — *TS 20 Jan. 97*

Responding to the rumor that the Super Bowl will be his last game as head coach of the Patriots: "Nothing has changed. Just because there is another report out doesn't make it different. I want to say this again: When the season is over, I am going to sit down with Bob Kraft and we're going to talk about it. That's not the issue here; the issue is the Green Bay Packers and New England Patriots in the Super Bowl." — *TS 21 Jan. 97*

Fourth Quarter
NY Jets Head Coach

Talking about one of the things he had in mind for his new team, the New York Jets: "We're going to find out who the bus drivers are. We'll see who's going to ride and who's going to get off." — *TS 25 Feb. 97*

Commenting on the abuse he absorbed from the Boston media after he left the Patriots to coach the Jets: "The way things are going up there, before too long, they'll be blaming me for the ball going through Buckner's legs." — *TS 5 Apr. 97*

Regarding his image as a callous figure: "I raised three daughters; there is some compassion." — *TS 12 Apr. 97*

On blending the styles of Jets 25-year-old receivers' coach Charlie Weis and 41-year-old quarterbacks' coach Ron Erhardt: "These young coaches have come up in pass-oriented situations, so in being around Ron and myself, Charlie's got exposure to both styles. What we're doing here is a combination of things we've done in the past and things we brought from New England. It's a hybrid." — *NYT 26 July 97*

On taking over the sad sack Jets: "Two guys are sent to Australia to sell shoes to the Aborigines. One calls his boss and says, 'there's no opportunities here; the natives don't wear shoes.' The other guy calls and says, 'there are a lot of opportunities here, these people don't have any shoes.' It depends on how you look at it. I think there's a lot of opportunity here." — *TSN 1 Sept. 97*

"I told the team I will not accept losing. I don't care if we're 0–14, I still won't accept it. And I don't want players that will." — *TSN 1 Sept. 97*

Parcells referred to LB Mo Lewis (who expanded to nearly 300 lbs.) as "a hunk of burning love." Lewis was motivated to drop 40 lbs. in 3 months. — *TSN 1 Sept. 97*

In response to TV analyst and former NFL coach Sam Wyche's prediction that the Jets would go on to claim the AFC East title: "I think Sam ought to lie on a couch and talk to somebody quietly, maybe with a little Mantovani playing in the background." — *TS 8 Sept. 97*

Assistant coach Bill Belichick after Parcells yelled at him for conducting a drill too close to a filming tower: "I pay him no mind. Bill suffers from prickly heat, which makes him cranky." — *SI 22 Sept. 97*

NFL's current crop of young offensive-minded coaches: "They don't know how to lead-block, counter, double-team; they don't have the background you need to create a solid running game." — *SI 22 Sept. 97*

After being asked by a reporter: "If you win the Super Bowl, will they rename the Meadowlands, Parcellsland?" Parcells responded: "Is LSD back?" — *SI 22 Sept. 97*

A sign in the Foxboro crowd during the "Tuna Bowl" vs. New England: "Go home Bill Par Sell Out." — *TS 23 Sept. 97*

On his search for replacements for his injured defensive linemen: "You put some of those heads on the end of a club and they look like a Volkswagen on a stick." — *TS 23 Sept. 97*

"Jeez! You've got this kid out in Canton already. He hasn't even made it to Harrisburg." Parcells' take on the press going crazy over Jets' impressive rookie kicker John Hall. — *SI 20 Oct. 97*

"We're trying to get this kid (Hall) off diapers and into his street clothes. Today, we took those Huggies off." — *TS 10 Nov. 97*

On how he deals with his disdain of black cats, which caused a major fuss within animal rights circles and saw him quoted, as follows, in *Animal Times*: "You know how to erase cats, don't you? If one goes across your car, you can drive over him. Then you can back up. Then, if you drive back over him, he's erased. I've done it." According to his attorney, Parcells was misunderstood. He really meant that his superstitious beliefs caused him to back up over the cat's "track," as opposed to the cat himself. — *TS 25 Oct. 97*

To linebacker Pepper Johnson who returned to the Jets' locker room after undergoing season-ending surgery: "Hey Johnson. You know what I'm going to do? I'm going to put two pictures on your locker. One's going to be of a beautiful sunset, with you in it. The other's going to be a picture of Evander

Holyfield. You figure out which one fits you — the retirement or the comeback." Johnson responded with a passionate and expletive-filled denial that he was ready to retire. — *SI 3 Nov. 97*

The Jets responded with a win after being "challenged" by their coach during the week's practices: "Sometimes you don't know why things happen. As discouraged as I was last week, now you have hope again. That's what makes this a great game. I'm as humble in this win just the same as I was in defeat last week." — *VV 23 Dec. 97*

First-day-on-the-job greeting to newly signed free agent RB Curtis Martin: "Hey, Boy Wonder, you better make me look good." — *TSN 15 June 98*

"Proactive" — Parcells' one word summation of his hard-line approach to coaching. — *TSN 17 Aug. 98*

After finding out he was on the cover of the December 14, 1998, issue of *Sports Illustrated*: "I requested purposely not to be on that cover. I took a photo with them with a guarantee that it would not be on the cover." — *Sun-Sentinel, South Florida 11 Dec. 98*

Phil Simms, former Giants QB under Parcells, and host of the Jets' weekly TV show was "kidded" by his former coach: "You've been riding on my back for so long, Simms, they should call me Ol' Paint." — *SI 14 Dec. 98*

Simms later mentioned that Parcells would be back on the show later in the season to do a promo for Thanksgiving. Simms: "We'll have another show to tape before Thanksgiving, right?" Parcells: "No we don't, Simms. This is the night we have to do it, Simms. Unless there's a different calendar for you than for everybody else." After shooting the acknowledgement that they have much to be thankful for, Parcells turned to the audience and snapped: "I almost said, 'and the thing I have to be most thankful for is that you're not playing quarterback for the New York Jets.'" — *SI 14 Dec. 98*

Former Giants QB, and Super Bowl hero Jeff Hostetler: "I have nothing but great things to say about the man as a coach, but I didn't enjoy one minute of my time with him. I know that sounds strange, but that's how it is when you're around Bill Parcells." — *SI 14 Dec. 98*

After a playoff loss a few years ago: "This game is going to kill me yet." — *SI 14 Dec. 98*

In response to a question from *Sports Illustrated*: "Well, if you were to ask my wife — and you won't be, by the way." — *SI 14 Dec. 98*

On his coaching style: "If you're sensitive, you will have a hard time with me." — *SI 14 Dec. 98*

"The only players I hurt with my words are the ones who have an inflated opinion of their ability. I can't worry about that. I'll call somebody 'dumb' or 'stupid' if they make a dumb or stupid play. I don't know any other word for it, and if they don't like the word, that's too bad." — *SI 14 Dec. 98*

"Mind Games? Look, I don't think about them. The ability I have as a coach is to see the end picture. I've been around enough to know what it takes to get a team to reach its potential, and I want players who want to reach their potential. Because I feel I can see the end picture, I'm less tolerant than I used to be, less tolerant of mistakes and players who aren't giving everything. I'll tell you when I knew that was the way I had to be: right after I almost got fired (following his rookie season with the Giants)." — *SI 14 Dec. 98*

On Mark Collins, a safety who starred on the Giants' 1991 Super Bowl win: "Maybe I got on him a little too much, went a little too hard. Maybe I never let him know what a good player I thought he was. But, you know, I ran into him recently and he said to me, 'Thank you for being the way you were. You made me a better player.'" — *SI 14 Dec. 98*

Parcells had this to say about colleague Buddy Ryan and his blunt coaching style: "Buddy had a philosophy, and he pursued it without fear, no fear!" — *SI 14 Dec. 98*

Parcells' take on the West Coast Offense that features the short passing game: "This idea came from all those offensive coordinators who want to be head coaches so bad." — *SI 17 Aug. 98*

On tight-end Kyle Brady who, after complaining about not being thrown to often enough thus far in his career, dropped a couple of balls in training camp: "I keep reading about all those opportunities you missed. There's two more you missed right there." — *SI 17 Aug. 98*

RB Keith Byars on Parcells: "There are Bill Parcells requirements for every position. The wide receivers have to be the guys who don't wear gloves and mittens on cold days. The running backs are the old down-and-dirty warhorses who could have played in any era." — *SI 14 Dec. 98*

Byers also says: "If he tells you there's cheese on top of the mountain, you'd better bring crackers." — *TS 31 Dec. 98*

NFL Syndicated Columnist Norman Chad saluted Parcells as follows: "It is a wonder of nature that caterpillars turn into butterflies. It is a wonder of Parcells that Vinny Testaverde has turned into Joe Namath." — *TS 24 Dec. 98*

Chad continues: "Parcells doesn't so much coach as he commands. When he says lights out at 11, you smash every light fixture by 10. If he told his players the Earth were flat, none of them would cross the street. He could stare at a blue sky so hard, it would become cloudy." — *TS 24 Dec. 98*

Regarding how smart a player should be under Parcells, an anonymous source had this to say: "Bill treats players as if they've got an IQ of about 95. You can't have a 70 IQ, and you can't have a 120. Of course, there are smart guys who figure it out and go the blue collar, don't-question-me route, like Simms." — *SI 14 Dec. 98*

Parcells often had soft spots for veteran players whom he felt could fill a specific need on his team. He contacted an out-of-shape and reluctant LB Bryan Cox in the off-season and encouraged him by stressing: "I don't care if you're ready on August 1. I want you ready on September 1." Cox was ready and played an important role on the Jets' defense in 1998. — *SI 14 Dec. 98*

Anonymous Source: "Bill knows it's impossible to control every element of the locker room, so he gets five or six players who speak the message for him and who are his eyes and ears and completely devoted to him." — *SI 14 Dec. 98*

After Parcells offered him the quarterback coaching position on the Jets, Jeff Hostetler (who chose to remain an active player with Washington) said: "It was one of the most flattering calls I ever got when he asked me to join his staff, because he had never given the slightest indication I had earned his respect when I was with the Giants. But I honestly don't know if I could work with him. He makes a lot of demands, and I don't know whether I could make that commitment. But if you do make the commitment, then you are a Parcells guy, probably for life." — *SI 14 Dec. 98*

According to Jets' WR Keyshawn Johnson: "I don't have a problem with taking orders and I don't think any other real players do. We just want to take the right orders from the right person, and that's what you get from Bill Parcells." — *SI 14 Dec. 98*

His theory on winning, as told to *ESPN Magazine*: "Winning doesn't feel as good as it used to and losing feels worse. This is my crack cocaine. I know it's like an assembly line, okay? And I know some day the line is going to stop, and that's when you're J-A-G. Just another guy." — *SI 17 Aug. 98*

"In the last three years, passers who threw for 300 yards in a game won 51 percent of the time. In the last three years, teams with a 100-yard rusher in the game won 70 percent of the time. So I say, Parcells, what's the smartest way to play? I'm just a phys-ed guy, but it seems pretty obvious to me." — *SI 17 Aug. 98*

After the 17–10 win in Buffalo that clinched the AFC East title, Parcells told his team: "You hear same old Jets, same old Jets. Well now you're the champs and nobody can take that away from you. You have a responsibility to keep playing that way." He later told reporters: "It's pretty emotional for me today, I can't even recount much of this game." LB Bryan Cox noted: "It was the first time he was at a loss for words, the first time we'd ever seen that." Parcells also commented: "When we were 0-and-2 this year, I didn't know if we'd ever win a game. There's still a lot to do. I don't think we're done." — *New York Daily News (NYDN) 21 Dec. 98*

"My players make me look good as a coach. My daughters make me look good as a father." — *Parcells, photo caption.*

"Sometimes you're a narc. Sometimes you're Dr. Joyce. And sometimes you've got to be a freaking journalism scholar. There ought to be a school someplace coaches could go to." — *Parcells p. 176*